MacR[...]
How to tra[...]
Scottish Ancestors

Tim Bede

Illustrations by
McCormick

Macdonald Publishers · Edinburgh

© Tim Bede, 1982

Published by Macdonald Publishers
Edgefield Road
Loanhead
Midlothian
EH20 9SY

ISBN 0 904265 68 4

Printed in Scotland by
Macdonald Printers Ltd
Edgefield Road
Loanhead
Midlothian
EH20 9SY

Contents

Chapter One — *Getting down to it*   **5**

Chapter Two — *Building up the trunk
and the main branches*   **12**

Chapter Three — *Tracking down the branches
and twigs*   **28**

Chapter Four — *Before 1855 — Baptisms, Banns,
Burials*   **33**

Chapter Five — *Adding the leaves and the flowers*   **39**

Chapter Six — *Long distance research*   **47**

Chapter Seven — *Now that you have got all that
material, what do you do with it?*   **58**

Appendix I — *New Register House Costs*   **66**
Appendix II — *Names and the Ancestor-Hunter*   **67**
Appendix III — *The regularity of irregular marriages*   **70**
Appendix IV — *Illegitimacy — a hurdle for the
ancestor-hunter*   **71**
Apendix V — *Other records in New Register House*   **73**
Appendix VI — *Specialists in Family Research*   **74**

Chapter One

Getting down to it

'The longest journey,' someone once said, 'begins with the first step' – and your search for roots, no matter how long it will eventually hold your attention, can begin at this very moment, in the comfort of your armchair at home. Reduced to its simplest, ancestry hunting is merely getting down on paper facts from three sources:

- **a.** Yourself
- **b.** Other people
- **c.** Printed information.

The first of these may be so obvious as to be taken for granted but there is no doubt that the work done from **a.** and **b.** is essential in terms of clarifying what it is you are setting out to do – and giving you the best start as far as tackling **c.** is concerned.

What do you know?

To start the ball rolling, scribble down on a large piece of paper just how you see you and your family fitting into any context of family networks. Try and keep all people in the same generation on a single level, ancestors above them, descendents below. Use some of the conventional abbreviations. For 'married' write = , for 'born' write **b**, for 'died' write **d**. Try and incorporate in your rough tree such details as occupation, location of main homes, maiden names etc.

Your chart will eventually develop into a very 'bottom-heavy' affair, with lots of aunts and uncles, nephews and nieces. The top half of the page will be comparatively sparse of branches. This is your mission: to extend the chart upwards and backwards in time, while at the same time trying to amass as much information as possible about the individuals who make up the chart.

The first way of adding to the information you have supplied out of your own head is to go and speak to other members of the family, who, because they are older or because they live nearer the family roots, will be better placed to extend your knowledge. Think specifically about who are the relatives best placed to provide this information. And don't restrict yourself to relatives; there may very well be long-standing family friends who might prove an even better source of information. No matter who you decide upon, contact them as soon as possible by visit or by letter. Tell them just what it is you are out to do and ask specific questions to get them started. You will have produced pointers to the blanks in your original doodlings. Spell these out in your conversation or letters. What was grandma's maiden name? Where did Auntie Nell go after she married? What regiment was Jimmy in?

MacRoots Tip

Get in touch with relatives and especially the elderly ones immediately. Their birth certificates will be around in ten years time—their memories, their family photographs and even they themselves may not be!

One important aspect will emerge at the earliest stage, perhaps even from your initial attempt at a family tree. The family tree itself is not enough to log all the material you will want to record. It is more a schematic index to what you are collecting rather than the collection itself. So develop a system of storing material which will run alongside the family tree and which will take into account all the detailed information. For example, you will soon have enough names and dates cluttering up the tree to make it impossible to incorporate all the details of your great grandfather's death. The event may be summed up in the tree by a mere date '1933', but somewhere you want to record that the death took place at 6 Church Row, Inverbirnie, that the cause was pneumonia, that the occupation was given as 'master builder' and that the information was provided by his nephew, James Dunbar.

There are two different approaches to recording this type of information. In one, each *individual* has a sheet/card of his own; in the other, each *family* has a sheet/card of its own. The one you plump for will be a decision for you. The first calls for many more information sheets and gives plenty of room for detailed information; the second is less extravagant and is ideal for showing family groupings and name patterns.

The illustrations show sample layouts for each type. From a typed original you may get duplicated copies at any centre offering this service. If you are getting duplicating done, don't skimp—order in hundreds rather than dozens for the first style, tens rather than units for the second. At this 'homework' stage, it is also important to start trying to track down any documents that exist in the possession of relatives. In some cases these may merely be the certificates which, as we shall

NAME ... *Alexander McFARLANE*

BIRTH/BAPTISM REGISTRATION *1791 Perth*

Date and place ... *26 Jan 1991. Perth*
Father ... *Thomas McFarlane, weaver in Pomerium*
Mother ... *Janet Glass*
Reported by/Witnesses ....

MARRIAGE/BANNS REGISTRATION *13 July 1819 Perth.*

Date and place ... *Dissenters Church, Perth.*
Address ... *Both of Pomerium, Perth*
Age and occupation ... *27, clerk*
Parents ... *As above*
SPOUSE *(1) Janet Hay   (2) Elizabeth Allen (see sep. sheet)*
Witnesses ... *Thomas McFarlane.*

DEATH REGISTRATION *1882. Edinburgh Canongate 18.*

Date and place ... *14 January 1882. 69 St Leonards, Edin.*
Cause of death ... *Old age, bronchitis*
Age and occupation ... *91 – Fire insurance agent*
Burial details ... *Newington Cemetery*
Reported by ... *John Bone – son in law.*
Parents ... *as above.*

CHILDREN

William	*Thomas*	
Andrew	*Alexander*	
Isabella	*Robina*	

CENSUS DETAILS

1841 *9 Davie St. Edin*	1871 *1 Gladstone Terrace*
1851 *3. W. Arthur Place*	1881 *69 St Leonards St.*
1861 *3. W. Arthur Place*	1891

also: Will + inventory
· PO Directories 1837-81

GENERATION BAND *6*

Family Group Sheet

	HUSBAND	WIFE
Name	ALEXANDER McFARLANE	JANET HAY

Birth
Date: 26 January 1791 / 21 August 1998
Place: PERTH / Perth

Baptised
Date: 28 January 1791 / 29 August 1798
Place: PERTH / PERTH

Married
Date: 13 July 1819
Place: Dissenters' Church, Perth.

Died
Date: 14 January 1882 / 12 May 1839
Place: 67 St Leonards, Edinburgh / Canongate Edinburgh

Father: Thomas McFarlane / John Hay
Mother: Janet Glass / Janet Muirhead
Other spouse: Elizabeth Allen (m

CHILDREN in order of birth

	Name	Date of birth	Date of marriage	Date of death
1.	William	1819		
2.	Andrew	1822		
3.	Isabella	1824		
4.	Thomas	1829		
5.	Alexander	1833		
6.	Robina	1838		
7.				
8.				
9.				
10.				
11.				
12.				

Notes on sources, testaments, law cases, trade directories etc

Will (see photostat) ; trade directories Edinburgh 1837-1881.

10

see, are available at New Register House. In other instances they may provide, in the shape of family bibles, prayer books, diaries, insurance certificates, property deeds and such like, information which will prove invaluable in your task.

MacRoots Tip

Don't neglect the humble copies of birth, marriage and death certificates. The more you can accumulate from private sources, the fewer you will have to track down in New Register House—and the more information you will have to identify precise lines of search.

Family photographs are especially treasured, as they offer a dimension which can rarely be equalled in the written word. And remember, any photographer worth his salt can make a fine copy of the most valued and fragile family photograph. They have even been known to improve upon the sepia original! When you have done all you can to extract information from dim and distant relatives, you are well prepared to make the lengthy step from personal reminiscences to public records.

Chapter Two

Building up the trunk and the main branches

Look at the chart on pages 14-15 of this book and you will see the barest of frameworks for a family tree – a bald, straightforward indication of your direct ancestors. It includes only the folk who have had a part in producing you, uncluttered by any brothers and sisters, aunts and uncles, the so-called *collateral lines*. We have left blanks for you to fill in your own details if you wish, for no matter how detailed a family tree you eventually hope to produce, this will provide the essential basic frame on which to build. Some of the spaces you will be able to fill in immediately, from your own knowledge or from the information collected from distant aunts or whoever. It is unlikely that you will be able to *complete* the chart from these sources, and at this point you need to get down to the documents. One store of goodies takes precedence over all others – over 120 years' worth of state records.

Births, Marriages and Deaths since 1855

Just after you were born, when your parents had eventually decided on the name or names that were going to accompany you as life-long dog-tags, one of them probably went along to the local Registrar and fed your details into the system. A similar procedure accompanies marriages, whether in Church or Registry Office, and deaths. This State responsibility for logging the comings and goings of its citizens has been carried on in Scotland since 1 January 1855. And the results of all that red-tape is an enormous store of all the original entries, indexed, maintained and at your disposal at New Register House, Edinburgh, and all for a small fee.

Before going on to explain how you get your hands on this information here are a few brief notes on what each type of certificate contains and what to look out for when you get to see the entries.

The Birth Certificate will tell you, in addition to the details you already know about the infant's name and sex:

* Date and place of birth—even down to the time of delivery. Pay special attention to the address—you may need it later to help you get at the Census returns.

* Details of the parents—occupation of father, maiden name of mother and *most vital* the place and date of the parents' marriage.

* Name of informant—not usually of importance as it is usually the mother or father, but where it is not one of these make a note of it—the information may very well come in useful later.

A Marriage Certificate will, as it relates to two people, be even more fruitful as far as information is concerned. It will tell you:

* Where and when the marriage took place and, when applicable, by which religious rites it was performed. Don't neglect to note this; you may be able to establish a family tradition of church-going which will be useful later on.

* Name, occupation, condition (bachelor or widower),

Your Ancestors

Record your direct ancestors on this chart. Give the full name, date and place of birth and death of each person, and the date and place of each marriage.

Father

b.

d.

Grandfather

b.

d.

m.

Grandmother

b.

d.

Self

b.

m.

Mother

b.

d.

Grandfather

b.

d.

m.

Grandmother

b.

d.

Great-grandparents	Great-great-grandparents	Great-great-great-grandparents
	m.	_____
	m.	_____
	m.	_____
	m.	_____
	m.	_____
	m.	_____
	m.	_____
	m.	_____

age and address of the bridegroom, together with name and occupation of father and name and maiden name of mother — essential information for the next generation step in your family tree.

* Similar details for the bride.

* Witnesses — take note of the people signing the certificate. In nine cases out of ten this information will be of little practical use, but in the tenth it could be a key link in your later researches. The signatures usually relate to the clergyman, a friend/relative of the groom and a friend/relative of the bride.

The Death Certificate is, unlike its counterpart south of the Border, a very valuable document in building up family trees. It will tell you:

* Name and occupation of the person whose death is reported — sometimes this occupation information is valuable as it may have changed (promotion, new job etc.) from the earlier information carried in the children's birth entries and such like.

* Details of any marriages — again a valuable detail, especially where it relates to earlier or subsequent marriages to the one you have been assuming.

* Where the death occurred — and when this happens away from the usual home, the regular address is also given. As in all instances, addresses are vital elements to be noted, both for the intrinsic value of knowing precisely where the people lived and for the "springboard" value of allowing you to plug into the Census information at a later stage.

* The age of the person — not always accurate, but a useful guide to the birth entry.

* Names of both parents, including occupation of the father and maiden name of the mother. This information, totally lacking from the equivalent document in England, provides the all-important lug on the jigsaw piece to enable you to make the next step backwards in your family tree.

* Cause of death — often rather technical in language but always worth recording. It sometimes includes details of the length of time that the dead person suffered from the complaint.

* The signature of the informant — the name of the person providing the information of a death tends to be more interesting than the names of the informant on other certificates. It can help you assess just how reliable the information is likely to be — it can also give you useful geneaolgical data. If for example, a Janet Robertson (maiden name Miller) has a death certificate signed by Hugh Wilson, brother-in-law, you can deduce that she had at least one sister and that that sister married a man called Hugh Wilson — a fair amount of information for a little column at the end of a death certificate!

These are the basic points to look out for in any of the standard certificates. Sometimes there will be even more information — notably in the 1855 entries which carried a wealth of data; sometimes there will be less — between 1856 and 1860 birth certificates did not include details of the parents' marriage.

These brief details will underline just what a wealth of information awaits you at New Register House. How do you make full use of that treasury?

New Register House is an elegant building at the east

end of Princes Street. It sits in the shadow of the more prominent Register House which faces along North Bridge.

MacRoots Tip

Don't neglect the first little column on the birth, marriage and death certificates. It indicates where an amendment to the original entry has been made and could lead you to a paternity suit, a bigamy charge or an enquiry into an accidental death. If there is a reference written in this column, ask the person showing you the entry where the relevant information is housed.

Paying in is a simple and not exorbitant affair. As New Register House is the home of a number of document stores essential to the genealogist and as the charges vary slightly according to which of these you want to look at, the scale of charges ranged from a basic £5.00 which allows you to get a day at the indexes of all those births, marriages and deaths which have taken place since 1855, to £90.00 which gives you three months of work among the full range of the statutory records, census returns and old parochial registers (about which more later). There are intermediate tickets available. Appendix I gives current charges. We are for the moment dealing with the state records of births, marriages and deaths and while in practice you will find it very valuable to be able to move from these to the other categories, for simplicity's sake we shall stick to those basic records. Let's imagine you have had a day to spare and want to use it to fill in some of those remaining blanks on pages 14-15. (It is, incidentally, a good idea to go for a day's 'familiarisation' before committing yourself to a week at the records.) Go to the reception area and fill in an application form for the facility you require — a day at the indexes of the statutory records. Payment of the appropriate fee will provide you with a reader's ticket and the freedom to consult the shelves of weighty indexes. Despite the rather overpowering number of indexes, the system is a simple and easily understood one.

Birth, marriage or death? The first division of the index volumes is into the three main categories — *Births* are all grouped together and indicated by red on the facing spines. *Marriages* are green and *Deaths* are black.

When? Within the broad groupings, the volumes are then shelved and marked by the year in which the event was recorded. (Sometimes there was a slight delay, so you may, for example, find a death that occurred near the end of 1877 being logged in 1878.)

Who? Male and female events are grouped separately so that, for example, the birth of twins, boy and girl, would be logged in different columns of the index in earlier years and in different parts of a combined volume in later years.

MacRoots Tip

When you are ranging through a large number of index volumes to track down an individual, pay particular attention to date and sex on the outside of the book to make sure you don't miss out a year or look at Female Deaths for 1888 missing the one you are really looking for in Male Deaths 1888.

Having determined the event, the year and the sex, you should be able to go straight to the relevant index and find the person you are seeking. Let's take a simple example.

You are looking for the death entry of your grandfather who, you believe, died in Glasgow in 1933. You go to the deaths indexes, find the volume for 1933 and, as it is one that contains records of all deaths, you turn to the section relating to male deaths.

You look up the surname and then go down the column looking for the matching first name/s. Unless

20

you are very clever and come up with a really special case, there are a number of fairly commonsense possibilities.

1. You find one and only one entry of that name, followed by the name of a Glasgow registration district and an identifying number. Lucky you — you seem to have made it! Note the details on your pad.

2. You find a number of entries for that name and a few of those are followed by the name of a Glasgow registration district. You have slight problems. At the worst you make a note of all contenders and try and track them down. At best you try and eliminate as many as possible. The one shown to be aged 27 is unlikely to be the grey-bearded ancestor you remember from the family photograph; the one who died north of the river cannot be your staunch southsider etc.

3. You find no-one of that name at all in the index. Solution: you may have got the date wrong; have a look in the years either side of 1933. You may have got the spelling of the name wrong — in many instances there is no real alternative, but if, say, you are a Miller, there is no reason to assume that your grandfather was not a Millar — or at least that the person giving the information to the Registrar thought he was!

Eventually, however, we shall assume that you get ideally one candidate or at the outside two or three. You must have a note of four elements to locate the unique entry relating to one person:

1. Birth, marriage or death?
2. The year.
3. The Registration District (given in the index) and

its reference number (shown on a wall chart in the index area).

4. The number of the entry in the Registrar's book (given in the Index).

Let us say from the example above we have a death, for 1933, in Glasgow Possilpark, number 111. How do we find just what information is carried in that entry? First the theory.

No-one has any right to examine the actual entries and the theoretical procedure at this stage — open to all — is to order an official copy of the actual entry, specifying all the identifying data mentioned above. On payment of a set fee, the staff of New Register House will copy details and forward them to you. If you are planning to get details from a large number of entries, this is a slow and expensive method. (It is the only one available — at higher rates too — to the searcher in England and Wales.)

The Registrar-General for Scotland has, however, mindful of the requirements of ancestor hunters, allowed individuals as a privilege to look at the actual entry and make notes from it *at no extra charge to the original access fee*. The holder of the office has been blessed by generations of hunters!

The procedure is simple. Having obtained all the data needed to single out the entry you are looking for, you put your name down on a waiting list kept at the counter on the index floor, and await your turn. When your name is called out by the Repository Assistant, you let him know what it is you are looking for. Death 1933, Registration District 645, Entry 111. He will take you up to the second floor (Deaths), will locate for you the relevant volume for the specified years and open it for you at the entry you have specified. You are then allowed to make what notes you wish. Using a pencil!

If you have two or three possibilities you may inspect each one. The information on the entry will — by indicating the occupation, the wife's name, etc — enable you to determine which one is yours. You then note all the relevant information on your pad.

MacRoots Tip

To simplify note-taking when you get to see the actual entry, why not rule out pages in your notebook in advance showing, for example, for a Death Certificate the key columns of place and date, age and occupation, name of wife, cause of death, father's name, mother's name, informant. It saves you time — and makes sure you don't miss anything out!

This information will allow you to return to the index floor and pursue the next line of investigation. Because of the very nature of the task, it is not always possible to clump together a number of entries when you are taking your turn with the Repository Assistant. Whenever you can, however, do so!

Exactly the same procedure is followed with a Birth or Marriage Entry, using the relevant indexes.

How, then, do you relate this approach to your own search for direct ancestors, the first target in our mission?

There is no infallible formula, as each family will have its very own characteristics, but a typical approach to the problem of filling in the basics as far as direct ancestors are concerned might be as follows:

1. Seek out the death certificates of your grandparents where you are reasonably certain as to when and where they died. These entries will give you the next stages as far as parents are concerned. If, however, you are uncertain of the death dates, but are reasonably sure of the dates on which your grandparents were married (children might remember wedding anniversaries, the birth of the youngest child might give an approximate date of the marriage etc) search instead for the *marriage* entry.

2. When you have obtained the names of your great-

MacRoots Tip

Go for the marriage entry wherever possible

a. Because two people are involved it gives you a choice of name to look up in the indexes — useful when one of the names is a common one and the other less common. If you have a William Robertson marrying Christian Auchterlony — look up Auchterlony — there won't be so much competition!

b. You kill two birds with one stone as you obtain from one marriage certificate the same information that would be carried on *two* death certificates, plus a few bonus details, e.g. witnesses, church, etc.

grandparents, repeat the operation to find their parents. At this stage, the best bet would usually be their marriage certificate. It may involve wading through a lot of indexes but you are more likely to find them that way than by hunting for two separate death entries. *Remember: the birth certificates of their children may give the place and date of the marriage, so think about that possible approach.*

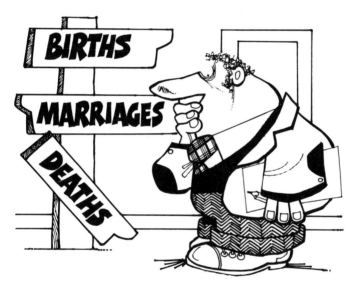

3. Carry on in this manner until you reach the Great Divide of 1855. Before that date there was no state recording of births, marriages and deaths and no information is carried in this particular section of New Register House. We shall come to the world beyond 1855 at a later stage.

There remains one important change of tack which is open to you to carry you a little or sometimes a long way beyond 1855. This involves switching back to the Death Certificate search. If, let us say, you have a pair of ancestors married in 1858, you clearly cannot find their parents' marriage entry (although you have their names) in the post-1855 records. Here, however, *if the 1858 marriage entry has not shown them to be deceased*, you can look for—with resignation to a long search in the index perhaps—their individual death entries which will give you the names of their parents.

MacRoots Tip

When looking for death entries of two married people, take a gamble and go for the man (unless he had a very common name); he is more likely to die first. When you have found this entry you can see whether his wife is already dead (in which case you can backtrack for her) or is still alive (in which case you have only later volumes to search through). Remember that the wife will be listed under both maiden and married names, however, and if she has a distinctive maiden name there may be an advantage in looking for her by that name—and of course checking under her married name in the same year to make absolutely sure you have the right one.

Such is the wealth of information carried in the post-1855 Scottish records that, although they were started *eighteen years* after the English and Welsh equivalents, they can, with a bit of average luck, carry the searcher well beyond 1800. A death entry of an ancestor expiring in 1858 for example at the age of 60 would take you backwards to a birth around 1798 and name parents who could have been born around 1770. It would not take exceptional luck to carry you back to the days of Bonnie Prince Charlie from a death certificate in the early years of state registration. Certainly, the records would, with a modicum of good fortune, allow the reader with a solid Scottish background to fill in much if not all of the chart on pages 14-15 from the well-indexed, centrally stored state records. We shall assume that you have been able to do so and return to the second task: to start filling in some of the smaller branches and even twigs of that impressive trunk and boughs which you have put together.

Chapter Three

Tracking down the branches and the twigs

If you have got hooked on the thrill of the chase (if that's not mixing a sporting metaphor), don't despair at the thought of leaving all those great-great-greats. We shall return to them at a later stage, but for the moment let us backtrack and start filling in some of the twigs and sideshoots of the family tree. It will help us to learn something more of the individual ancestors you have already traced—and will stand us in very good stead when we come to push that line of direct ancestors back still further.

We could, of course, track down all the sisters and aunts, the side branches of the tree, using much the

same techniques that we have employed in tracing the direct ancestors. But there is a much more effective way of building sideways — the Census returns.

Counting Heads 1841-1891

Just as central government took over responsibility for noting the major personal events of birth, marriage and death to keep tabs on just what was happening to the population, so at about the same time, it became concerned with counting heads and taking details of the entire population. The first headcount took place in 1801 and thereafter at regular ten-yearly intervals, with the exception of 1941, until the latest in 1981. For the ancestor hunter, however, there is a chunk of six censuses from 1841 to 1891 that are especially significant. The returns for those years are kept at New Register House and are available for consultation. Next to the enormous wealth of 126 years of state-noted births, marriages and deaths, the availability of six censuses detailing every person living in Scotland on a specific census night (there were over 2½ million at the 1841 census) is the greatest fund of information for the ancestor hunter.

What do the census returns tell you — and how do you find your way to the information?

The amount of information varies considerably from census to census. At the beginning, the 1841 Census asked for a limited amount of data — names, approximate ages, occupations, whether the person was born in the parish, elsewhere in Scotland or outside Scotland. By 1851, the questions were asking for such details as relationships to individuals within a household, precise ages and, vital for later searches, the actual parish of birth. By 1891, the censuses had passed through a number of extra questions, including the ability to speak Gaelic, the number of rooms being shared by the families and, relevant in a small number of cases, evidence of disabilities.

The unit of the Census was the family and the home. The benefit of the first was that it brings to the researcher complete or partly complete family groups enabling him to build sideways from the main trunk. The disadvantage of the second element is that in order to get into the information you must know exactly where your family was living on a specific night once every ten years.

MacRoots Tip

Whenever you are making notes from census returns, take a look at the details of the neighbours. Jot down just who are sharing the front door with your ancestors, or farming alongside them or keeping the shop next door. The returns enable you to learn much more than the bare list of names, occupations and ages of your own forebears. It tells you a lot about the activities of a small localised neighbourhood.

How can you get hold of the information? Look back at the details you have collected in building up the main trunk of your family tree. Do any of the dates occur close to the census years of 1841, 1851, 1861, 1871, 1881 or 1891? If they do, start there. Let us suppose that you have details of a marriage which took place in 1873.

That would have given you *two* addresses (bride and groom) which may have been occupied by the families in 1871.

The census returns are kept in a different part of New Register House and it is possible to pay a fee which covers both the indexes and the census search. But this time the indexing system is very different — and the search element much greater. Let us suppose that you have identified addresses in Perth. You consult the indexes to the census returns to find out exactly what is the reference number for the enumerators' returns for Perth. Here luck has a large part to play. You might have a small village which would have been easy to cover, going straight through the columns looking for your address. At the other extreme you may have had Edinburgh or Glasgow, where indexes for specific streets would have been available. Instead you have landed with the more difficult middle situation. You fill in a form requesting the returns for Perth and are given a pile of books to search through. You are only looking for a specific street — so concentrate on the address column looking for, say, Canmore Place. It could be the first page you turn to; or you could find it half an hour and some wobbling eyes later.

Once you have found the street, it is usually not difficult to find the house — although numbering of houses is not a universally practised art amoung enumerators! Then if you are in luck you could land up with something like the following, an actual example taken from research such as you are involved in.

Robert Hay, Head, 47, wine merchant, born Aberdour, Fife

Jane Pringle Hay, wife, 47, born North Queensferry,
Fife
Christina Hay, 23, daughter, born Inverkeithing, Fife
Jessie Hay, 21, daughter, born Inverkeithing, Fife
Robert Hay, 14, son, general merchant apprentice,
born Leith
William Hay, 9, son, scholar, born Edinburgh.

Just think of the tremendous amount of information
carried in that entry — and in particular look at the
evidence of the family's movements contained in the
birth places of the children!

All your work has been worthwhile and you have been
rewarded with a mine of genealogical information and
family details.

MacRoots Tip

The value of the Census lists in building up
quick 'growth' is so great that you should set
out to find exactly where your forebears were
for each of the years for which the returns are
available. To do so you may have to get
information closer to the dates than that
collected so far. Try trade directories (see
page 42) or look for entries closer to the key
dates for brothers and sisters of your direct
ancestors.

The census returns enable you to tag on a large
number of brothers and sisters of the people you have
traced in Chapter Two — and enables you to do this at
high speed, with appropriate dates of birth (don't take
census ages as gospel!), with details of occupations and
apprenticeships, lodgers and servants.

Chapter Four

Before 1855 — Baptisms, Banns and Burials

The great date for any ancestor hunter in Scotland is 1855, the year in which the State took unto itself the responsibility for noting the birth, marriage and death of each of its citizens. Before that time, no-one had undertaken these charges.

The events did, however, coincide with three major religious happenings in the Church — the baptism of an infant, the sanctifying of a marriage and the interment of a follower. The Church records of these events are the closest we get before 1855 to the total logging which occurred afterwards. But before you cry 'Yippee' and start off on your pre-1855 quest, there is a load of bad news for anyone expecting to find pre-1855 Church records in any way approximating to the post-1855 state records.

To grasp the nettle as firmly as possible, here is the bad news:

1. There was no firm directive to the Church as to how the records should be kept — information for any specific event varies wildly from parish to parish, from clerk to clerk.

2. There was no directive as to how long the records should be kept — in many many parishes for many many years there are no records whatsoever still in existence.

3. Not everyone felt obliged to have their children's birth, their own marriage recorded. In many instances it did after all cost money. In the Canongate records, the

logging of the baptism of an aristocrat's heir is crossed angrily out because the father refused to pay the Clerk's fee! In the Kirkcaldy records, the clerk bemoans the effect which a new stamp tax is having on parents as far as getting their offspring entered is concerned.

4. Comparatively few graveyards kept an informative record of burials.

5. There is no central index available to the individuals covered in the parish records which do still exist.

After that despairing news, a few silver linings would not come amiss. All of the existing old parish records have been transferred by the Church of Scotland to New Register House for safekeeping — and unlike your counterparts south of the Border it is not necessary to trot off to each individual parish in order to consult the records.

Secondly, a number of Session clerks were conscientious in their record-keeping, sometimes supplying considerable detail (one fine soul in Dundee includes in the baptism a note of the person after whom the child is named) and sometimes providing a helpful running index which provides a guide to the searcher.

Although the records for this new treasury — returns from more than 900 parishes housed in 4000 volumes — are again housed in New Register House, the route to the records is different from that so far described. In the case of the state records, you needed the names of an individual to open the door of the cupboard; in the case of the census returns you needed an address: now, you have to know the name of the parish in which your forebears were baptised, married and buried. *Without this information the task of getting anything from the old parish records is an almost impossible one.*

You will, however, have been given a clue as to which parishes are likely to be involved from:

a. *The state records* — these should have indicated some family 'base' and especially in the case of events occurring just after 1855.

b. *The census returns* — two censuses took place (in 1841 and 1851) before the introduction of state records, and are especially useful. Later censuses included in the information the name of the parish in which individuals were born — a key clue for hunters.

Once you have focused on a specific parish, the procedure is straightforward, even if the search may be long. Let us assume that you have located a number of your forebears in the parish of St Vigeans in Arbroath in

35

the years after 1855. On the shelves of the Library at New Register House there are two volumes relating to the Old Parochial Records (OPRs). From the index at the end of each volume, you can track down the number allocated to St Vigeans. The number in this case is 319 and the relevant book will be volume one which covers numbers 1-459.

Turning to the page referred to St Vigeans, you will see a complete list, with reference numbers, of all the records of baptisms, marriages and burials held for that parish. Decide just what it is you are looking for — maybe births of individuals listed in Census returns with approximate years to be looked at indicated by the ages given there. If, for example, you want to see whether any of the children born between 1850 and 1854 were recorded you request on the printed slip provided to see the relevant book. And thereafter it's a long or short search.

Often — increasingly often in fact — you will be supplied with microfilm records of the parish books, a careful step to preserve frail documents which for many years were made available to searchers with subsequent wear and illegibility. Don't be deterred by the technology — the staff will helpfully demonstrate the technique and you'll soon get used to it.

There are specific elements to look for in the OPRs which were not present in the state records. In the early baptisms for example, names of witnesses were often recorded. Make a note of these as there are often unexpected clues hidden away there — and in the sparse years before 1855 any little bit helps. Each witness, invariably male, usually represented one specific parent, and it is sometimes possible to corroborate certain relationships from the names, occupations and addresses of witnesses.

The most common feature of the OPRs, however, is

just what they omitted rather than what they included. You will be very lucky indeed if you come across names of parents (the essential pointer to the next generation) other than in the baptismal entries. They are normally not mentioned in marriage records and when they are, are usually limited to the father of the bride. They never seem to be mentioned on burial entries except in the case of young children.

A useful addition to the information carried in the OPRs is the excellent collection of gravestone inscriptions to be found on the Library shelves at New Register House. These have been collected over the years by avid enthusiasts trudging through thick grass in all corners of Scotland.

The parish records represent the last of the great sources of documentary evidence housed in New Register House, although other minor collections are listed in Appendix V. At this stage progress backwards in time becomes very difficult and, indeed, often impossible, and we should perhaps turn our attention not to extending the branches of the family tree, but to putting some more leaves and flowers on it by way of collecting some more detailed personal information about the ancestors we have collected so far.

Chapter Five

Adding the leaves and flowers

It may very well be that you are content enough to amass ancestors without any real desire to go beyond the name, rank and number level—the bare minimum of birth and death, parentage and offspring, home and occupation. But if so, you would be a very unusual person indeed. The desire to get some feel for the life and character of the people involved is a powerful one and, while it is far more difficult to track down this type of information as opposed to the logging of births, marriages and deaths, the quest for this information can be the most rewarding aspect of family research. Unlike the work on registrations, there are no basic guide lines to finding your way to any material which exists. Every family will have different avenues to pursue, according to where their ancestors lived, what they did, whether or not they owned land, whether or not they fell foul of the law.

Here is a brief and very incomplete list of some of the typical sources of material which might be explored by anyone aiming to put leaves and maybe flowers on his family tree.

1. Wills and testaments

All copies of Scottish testaments (and inventories of the estates to which they refer) are kept at the Scottish Record Office in Register House, the imposing building at the side and to the front of New Register House. Because of the astonishing variety of the material housed there, the simple all-embracing index system of New Register House is impossible and getting to grips with the indexes is a much more daunting task. (As compensation, a reader's ticket is free and you are asked to give a brief description of the purpose of your searches to enable staff to assist you.) While in general the existence of a testament is related to wealth and possessions, there are many instances of people with meagre possessions paying great attention to spelling out just what they want to happen to those goods when they pass on. So, if your forebears appeared to be poor people, do not rule out the chance of a juicy and informative testament awaiting you in the depths of New Register House. Some of the testaments may be dreary in the extreme and couched in legal jargon, but persevere and you could well come up with some gems of family history. But to make sure you are not going to waste time chasing up the wrong people, you must have done your homework well as far as building up your

MacRoots Tip

If a testament provides a particularly mouthwatering collection of facts, why not get a photostat made of it to keep with your notes. The photostat service offered at the Record Office is speedy and reasonably priced. It is especially useful for old, complicated documents which you can then unravel in the comfort of your own home.

family tree is concerned as every detail can help you to benefit from this store.

2. Registers of Sasines

Testaments in Scotland related only to moveable wealth. Ownership of land was catered for in voluminous Registers of Sasines. In order to find out just what exists in this store, it is essential that you know which of your ancestors owned which land and at which date. (Incidentally the Registers are concerned with owners and not tenants.)

3. Services of Heirs

When a person died in Scotland it was necessary for his heir to prove in court his right to succession. The chronicling of the court findings as far as succession is concerned is, after 1700, well indexed, providing extracted information which can be of help in filling in details of the family situation and even in identifying relationships which your earlier work had suggested but not established.

4. Court Cases

Without doubt, you will give thanks to any of your ancestors who fell foul of the law, for that gives you a chance to come across the old and dusty papers relating to his case. These can often provide a cascade of information, throwing an unexpected light on someone who was little more than a bundle of dates and addresses. Again, while the high and mighty with more to protect than most indulged in the most regular litigation, you will be surprised to find that people of all classes, from prince to pauper, found their way into the

41

files. Court cases detail arguments over a horse that died the day after the plaintiff bought it, workmen complaining even in those days of unfair dismissal, tenants protesting at a landlord's refusal to mend a roof. An especially fascinating source of information relates to bankrupts who were at first thrown into jail and were then required to make out a case for release (a Condescension) in which they outlined at great length

the business and family conditions which led to them being in that financial state. So keep your fingers crossed and hope for a bankrupt up the tree! The indexes for the court cases are huge and haphazard, but a few hours of browsing is well worth while!

5. Trade directories

Started for the larger urban centres in the second half of the eighteenth century, trade directories at first were concerned very much with the gentry and the professional men. Rapidly they came to be service guides, very much the Georgian Yellow Pages of Scotland, where you could find a pastrycook or a cowfeeder, a surgeon or an artificial leg-maker. Selections of these directories will be available at the big reference libraries (and indeed at the libraries you have already been using at New Register House and Register House), but the really fine runs will be held in the relevant area library — for example the Edinburgh Room at Edinburgh Central Library will be the place to go if you are looking for a continuous set of Edinburgh & Leith street directories, the Mitchell library if you are focussed on Glasgow.

The information carried in these directories is enormous. They usually list people alphabetically, by street and by occupation. Bear in mind the following points:

* The directories are trade publications — they may therefore throw more light on what your forebears did than the civil registration did.

    The later street directories even give a person's employer in many instances. An insurance clerk may have the information 'Sun Fire' added in brackets, the printer may have his publication added.

* Trade directories may often give a person's trading address *and* his home address. This can provide a useful guide to, for example, the extent or growth of a person's business. I followed the progress of a pharmacist from one shop (1865 directory) to five shops (1876 directory) in this way.

* Trade directories go much lower down the scale than even census returns do — and in particular often give the jobs of women — where these are not specified in either census or registration returns. A person who was never more than a mother-and-wife statistic in the OPRs appeared as a sick-nurse in the street directory.

* Trade directories often go well beyond the boundaries of the city to take in small townships on the outskirts and country gentry. Check this.

* Directories usually carried additional advertising — take a look at these announcements, especially if the person you are tracking was in the type of self-employed business that needed promotion.

* Directories carried a great deal of additional information on, say, delivery charges within the city. Take a look at these pages.

6. Lists of graduates and students

Universities and schools have published useful directories which provide information that often goes much further than one would expect.

7. The Ministers of Scotland

If you are very lucky, one of your ancestors will have been a minister in the Church of Scotland. Of all the professions, this is one which is arguably the best documented from the genealogist's point of view. The great *Fasti Ecclesiae Scotiae* details in many volumes the ministers ordained by the Church over the centuries. The entries seek to provide as much information as possible not only on the man's service within the Church but also on his family.

44

8. Session Books

Keeping with the Church, it is worth mentioning that in some areas the Session Books, mainly referring to the earlier period before 1855 civil registration, have been printed by local interests—and offer a much easier way of delving into the doings of your eighteenth-century ancestors. This is where the librarian will come in handy, knowing from your information which areas you are interested in. The local libraries are understandably the most likely source of this type of publication. If you can find a publication for the parish in which your forebears lived you may very well find them mentioned in the pages, either as the elders dispensing moral judgments, or as parishioners at the receiving end of charity or punishment (the pages are packed with moral pronouncements on backsliding among the faithful, generally as regards sexual relations!).

9. Scotland under the minister's eye

Perhaps the finest work to come from a Church source was the massive *Statistical Account*, the brainchild of Sir John Sinclair. In the late 1700s, anxious to produce a definitive study of Scotland (he was an agriculturist, businessman and imaginative thinker), he asked every parish minister in Scotland to produce a survery of his parish (Sinclair produced guidelines as to what they should look for)—and the result of this enormous undertaking is to be found in most large libraries in Scotand. (The success of Sinclair's venture can be judged by the fact that subsequent Statistical Accounts have been carried out from time to time, using a very similar basis for their scope and treatment).

By this stage, you will certainly have identified the parish in which your ancestors lived. You will also, if things have gone with even average smoothness, have got back to the sort of period (1790s) when this first Statistical Account was being prepared. You are now offered a thumbnail sketch (sometimes quite a hefty thumbnail) of exactly what was happening in that very parish. How much were the labourers paid? What equipment was used on the farms? What crops were grown? What factories existed? You will even find that the minister (and incidentally the quality of reporting varies considerably with the ability and dedication of individual clergymen) was even asked to list the worthies and famous men born in the parish. Values change, and the famous men listed in 1790 are not necessarily the ones who are known now. You may even find that someone whom you considered an unknown ancestor was in fact a famous ancestor.

Chapter Six

Long-distance research

Scots seem to have made their way to more numerous, more distant shores than almost any other nationality, and the result of this and that habit of setting up Caledonian Societies is that there are people from every corner of the world who see themselves as Scottish and their roots as undeniably tartan.

For them, the main theme of this book — the mouthwatering treasures that await them throughout the length and breadth of Scotland, and at the east end of Princes Street, Edinburgh, in particular — may seem a little irrelevant. This chapter is written especially for them — and indeed for many Scots who cannot get down to Edinburgh.

Even if you are doing it from a distance, the principles outlined in this book remain valid.

The first step is to find out as much as possible from your own sources. In particular, look out for specific and clearly dated links with Scotland.

When did your ancestor leave Scotland? Arrive in your present country? Do you have any records which can help to answer these points?

In addition to the family interviews/letters mentioned in this book, think in particular of the following:

1. Are there any records in my present country which give details of the Scottish link?

* A will made in Australia by your grandfather may mention brothers and sisters still left in Scotland.

* Scots leaving home in the nineteenth century were not required to file any details here in Scotland. Catching a boat across the ocean was no different, as far as Government records were concerned, from catching a bus today. Records do, however, often exist at the other end. Ships passenger lists were often filed at the port of entry. Governments often kept records of immigration, which can compensate for Scotland's lack of emigration records.

* Death records of, say, a Scot who came to Canada and died there may carry the name of his parents. If so, this is a very valuable piece of information, along with any details of his place of birth. (These are details which may even have been carried in the immigration records.)

48

MacRoots Tip

Some of the countries to which Scots emigrated in large numbers have produced valuable publications on the incomers. So if you live in Canada or the USA, New Zealand or Australia, check at your reference library to find out just what exists.

2. Are there any less formal clues to the Scottish connection?

* Scots often named their house in the new home after a farm or village or area where they lived in Scotland. Any record of your forebears' first years in their new home may indicate this.

* Are there any family traditions which could throw a light on Scotland? For the most part the bulk of family traditions are poor guides to reality, but it is not always the case. Often, an important element is handed down by word of mouth and where the details are precise enough this can be a help.

3. Are there documents which bridge the gap between Scotland and the new home?

Books? Diaries? Photographs? Old photographs may not have a background which will enable you to locate the setting, but commercial photographers usually have their mark somewhere on the surround or even back of the print.

4. Did you know anything of the family that were left behind?

Let us suppose that your grandfather came from Scotland and died in New Zealand and that his records in New Zealand give no indications of this parents or birthplace in Scotland. Did he have any brothers or sisters who did not go to New Zealand with him? What were their names? Were they older or younger than he was? More importantly, do you have any precise details of when they married? Or when they died? If you knew that his sister Isabella died in Dundee in 1897, that information would enable you to get from the Scottish records the same information as if your grandfather had died there.

5. Do you know anything of the Church to which your Scots ancestor belonged?

There was usually a tradition of church-going which passed on from parents to children. Particularly when looking back beyond the civil records, it is important to know which church was likely to have kept records of Births, Marriages and Deaths. As I have mentioned, the established Church of Scotland records are the ones kept by the Registrar-General in his old, pre-1855 material.

6. What was the profession or trade of your Scots ancestor?

This could provide one of the most valuable guides to tracking down a family (and not only in helping confirm that the Ian Macleod you track down is the same one that you knew about in Nova Scotia!). The professions have their own very fine directories, so that if the emigrating Scot was a doctor, minister or lawyer, you have a very good chance of finding him. Similarly, if he attended university in Scotland, it would be handy to see what information is carried on him in the directories of graduates. The same would apply to any school directories which may exist.

It is not only the professions, however, for whom there are fine, informative records. The Army records housed in London, provided you have some idea of the regiment, can give much information of value to the ancestor-hunter. Moreover, almost every trade or occupation found its way into the town directories which cover most of Scotland's cities from the early 19th century onwards. So if your ancestor was a bookseller or coachhirer, a bootmaker or a policeman, in Dundee or Glasgow, Edinburgh or Perth, this is invaluable as an aid to tracking him down.

MacRoots Tip

A number of Scots immigrants retained strong links with the home country by sending their children to one of the four great Scottish universities of St Andrews, Aberdeen, Glasgow and Edinburgh, at the peak of their international reputations in the nineteenth century. Check the graduate directories.

---

7. Did the family own any land, no matter how small, in Scotland?

The great Sasine registers list the owners (but not the tenants) of all land in Scotland. If you have a date and an address, it is possible to extract information from the Sasines which could help build up extra information on your family. The main aim of all this activity is to build up as much information as possible on your Scottish links, because the quality and quantity of the information which it is possible to extract from the records depends to a large extent on just what information you start with.

To tap the three great hoards of information held at New Register House, the following requirements are essential:

1. Births, Marriages and Deaths after 1855

To get to an entry you need a name and date, for a birth, a marriage or a death. A place would also help out, as would occupation or names of parents. These extras are important when the name is a common one.

2. The Census returns, 1841-1891

You must have a family name and an address which is applicable at or near one of the decennial census dates.

3. Pre-1855, Old Parochial Records

You must have in addition to family names and approximate dates a parish in which the baptisms, banns and burials took place.

Without these basic details, the chances of a successful search are eliminated or severely reduced.

But let's get back to the campaign. You, sir, there in Moose Jaw, or you, madam, sunning yourself in Lochinver! How can *you* get all this ancestor-hunting under way?

1. Ancestors by post

You can build up a wealth of information, by ordering, from the Registrar-General, copies of all the key documents which are needed to build up your family tree. This is:

a. *Expensive* — you, unlike the searcher on the spot who can take notes from a record, have to purchase a copy of the document. The charges are reasonable (you'll find them listed in Appendix I) but they mount up.

b. *Slow* — you have to wait for two postal services (you to the Registrar-General, he to you) with a searching and processing time in between. You usually can't get on with the next stage until you have noted the details carried on the first document.

c. Dependent on accurate information — the Registrar-General's staff are not involved in the business of research. They will find for you and copy an entry for which you provide enough information to make its location feasible. If you want a death certificate of George Macrae, who died in Inverness in 1876, they will provide it. If you want a certificate for a George Macrae who died somewhere north of Inverness, between 1870 and 1878, they are less likely to provide it.

Nevertheless, this is a feasible means of setting about the initial research. And it does have the benefit of providing you with copies or photostats of the actual documents which log your ancestors' history.

2. Using the professional searchers

If the staff of the Registrar-General are not in the business of personalised ancestry research, there are others who are — providing the on-the-spot investigation, speeded one may add by an expertise and flair for the records which cannot be acquired overnight for people who want to find out more about their Scottish roots. Naturally, with the concentration of most records in Edinburgh, this is very much a capital city profession!

Some of the professional searchers are listed in Appendix VI. If you want to enlist the aid of one of these experts, write to them with your task and come to some agreement on a maximum fee beyond which they will not proceed without your consent. £80 or £100 would be a reasonable figure. What are you going to get for that money?

There is, as you may have guessed from this book, no way of answering that question in advance. In essence the researchers are trying to build up one line only (the paternal) unless you ask otherwise (and that costs more). They will, for example, try and track down your great-grandfather's brothers and sisters, but not his in-laws.

The elements which influence just what you will get for your money are numerous but mainly the following:

1. *Information*: the more detailed and precise the information you can give, the more likely is it that the searchers will come up with a lot for that £80.

2. *Luck*: luck plays a key role in these searches — unusual names and, in the earlier records, the quality (or even existence) of parish records.

3. *Family size*: your searchers aim to track down the

paternal line and all children of each direct descent marriage. Now if you, sir, in Moose Jaw come up with a great-grandfather who had thirteen children, and you, madam, in Lochinver, with one who had only one child—your grandfather—then there are two likely sequences:

* You, sir, will get a large number of relatives on your list, but may feel a little disappointed at the number of generations the searchers have managed to get through.

* You, madam, may be very pleased at just how many generation bands the searchers have turned up, but a little disappointed at the lack of 'breadth.'

The tall spindly family tree or the dense squat family bush—you will certainly get a lot of effort from the searchers and they will be trying their hardest to make sure you are pleased with what you get for your money.

Incidentally, if the searchers comes up with an 'ancestor' that they cannot fix categorically from documentary evidence, they will end the search and let you know how things stand. You may then accept that while the link cannot be proved it is highly probable — and ask them to continue from the 'ancestor.'

MacRoots Tip

The professionals will be ranging over a very wide span of records, not only the births, marriages and deaths, but also legal, land and testamentary material, plus the many directories of apprentices and tradesmen, gravestones and school-rolls. You will get value for money in most cases.

---

3. A combination of 1 and 2

It is also worth considering a combination of 1 and 2, where this is possible. You deal directly with the Registrar-General, ordering key documents and building up a partial family tree which you can at some stage hand over to the professionals for their contribution.

All the very best of luck with your attempts to do it from a distance. You will certainly enjoy the experience and it may encourage you, sir, to make that trip from Moose Jaw to Scotland. And you, madam, in Lochinver, may think it worth coming down to Edinburgh for a couple of days after all.

Chapter Seven

Now that you have got all that material, what do you do with it?

Over the weeks (months? years?), you will have amassed an enormous hoard of information and at the end of asking a thousand and one questions of who, when and where, you are left with only two: when do I stop, and what do I do then?

The first is perhaps the simplest because there is no real answer to it. Genealogy is a jigsaw puzzle which gets bigger and bigger and which never throws up a piece with an unequivocal straight edge to let you know you've reached the end. And so there is always a temptation to keep searching. At some stage you must resist that temptation and say to yourself: I have reached the stage where I have so much information that I must try and get it down on paper in a manageable form as a record that can clarify my work from my own point of view and that can pass on the fruits of that work to others. Console yourself with the knowledge that this is not an irrevocable decision and any facts which come to light afterwards can be incorporated in all but the most polished version.

So you've decided to start getting it all down. Pay particular attention to three key aspects:

* putting in order the material you have

* incorporating it into the family tree

* producing a write-up of your findings

Putting in order the material you have collected

The tidy-minded worker will have been keeping a pretty close track of what material he has been accumulating. Now is the time for everyone to try and shuffle those sheets into a logical order, file all the census returns together, mark any cross references on your family or individual sheets. Now is also the time when you should take a careful look at your notepads and information sheets to see if you have missed out any details in transcription or if there are still gaps which can be easily filled.

Building up the family tree

Again, most of you will have been slowly building up a family tree, keeping it simple, using lines and abbreviations as you have seen in the examples in this book. It is now time to try and incorporate all of your material into what is still the most effective way of displaying genealogical information. Each family will pose its own problems as far as layout is concerned, but take a look at history books in your local library and see how other people tackle these challenges.

Get your roughs together and get a clear picture of what your end result should look like. Look at some of the history books at your local library and see how they tackle family trees.

MacRoots Tip

When it comes to producing the family tree, keep it simple. You are out to produce a device for registering and displaying information. You are not in the business of producing wall-paper, so cut out the symbolic branches and leafy excesses.

If you intend doing the tree yourself, bear in mind that the job calls for neatness, patience and dedication as much as artistic inspiration. It also calls for some pretty large sheets of paper. If you have any difficulty in local stationers or artists' materials shops, try any local businesses that you think would be handling such sheets—architects, drawing offices, and, best of all, printers especially of newspapers who have ideal layout sheets which they may part with in return for courtesy and a smile.

Modern fibre-tip and allied pens provide some ideal

writing implements—but check for permanence as you don't want your family tree to dissolve spectacularly when Aunt Mildred weeps over it in memory of her sister Jessie's details. If you are in the slightest doubt, go for the old well-tried Indian ink. You will also find that sticking to black ink will pay dividends when it comes to reproducing copies for distribution within the family.

MacRoots Tip

There may be other members of the family who have the necessary skills of lettering, drawing or writing that would complement the talents for research that you must have displayed. Collaborate where you think this might produce a better end-result.

The family history takes shape

You have gathered from the bald facts of birth, marriage and death the framework, the skeleton, for your family history. You should also somewhere along the line have been fitting that history into the events of the community and nation in which it took place, with local papers, census returns and such like filling in the details of the grass roots activity and the broader history books telling you something of what was happening in the world around.

You are now ready to build that information into narrative which can be read with interest by other members of the family or (and don't be modest) by people wanting to learn something about a tiny little segment of Scotland's history as represented by one family.

The easiest (and dreariest) thing in the world is to rattle off a list of births, marriages and deaths. Take a look at some of those chapters in the New Testament on the lineage of Jesus and you will be reminded that a chorus of begats is a powerful lullaby indeed.

The following are a few guidelines which might help those of you who are perhaps unused to writing a lengthy and continuous report of this type:

* While it may be that the right way to handle your family history is to start at the earliest date and work through to the present day, take a look at your family tree and see if there is an alternative. You may for example have found far more about one generation than another. If that is Generation Band Six, say, but you had actually traced the family back to Band Ten, don't waste time getting to the interesting bit. Start

with your key person and sketch in his background as a sort of flashback.

* The more you know about Scotland and its history, the better placed you are to slot your forebears into a period, so try some extra background reading now that you know where your forebears lived and what they did. Try and imagine someone in two hundred years' time trying to piece together a history of a family living in Clydeside in the 1940s and not knowing about World War II—and make sure that that is not what you are trying to do when you look back two centuries.

* Get to know something about the community in which your family lived. Local newspapers for the nineteenth century and the *Statistical Account* for the eighteenth should get you started.

* If you know something of your forebears' occupations, try and find out about what was happening in that trade. Weavers or locomotive-builders, farmers or builders—there are very few people indeed who were working at a job that has been neglected by the academics, writers and publishers of the twentieth century.

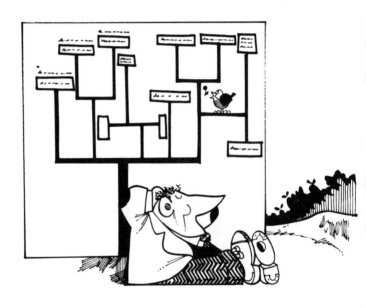

It may be that you really have difficulty in getting all this together; the amount of information can often deter even the most experienced writer. Again, look at the possibility that someone in the family may have a bent for narrative and a feeling for history. Collaborate with enthusiasm for the sake of the end product.

Finally, just imagine for a moment that you discovered in a dusty chest a bundle of sheets on which your great-great-grandfather had written a synopsis of his life: his childhood and friends, games and schools, work and courtship, holidays and hobbies, wife and children. Just feel the glee and ponder. You cannot 'create' that treasure that never was, but you can start laying it down for future generations. Set to it and prepare for the family history the contribution which you can make more fully than anyone in the world — the story of *your* life, a plain, but not too plain, collection of what you would like your great-great-grandson to know about you. Nothing too grand, not a great autobiographical novel. Although, if you do get hooked. . . .

Appendix I

New Register House costs at Summer 1981

A member of staff will search for a specific entry for you — when you have enough information to make identification likely. Any entry from the post-1855 Births, Marriages and Deaths, from the Old Parochial Records or the census returns can then be copied for you at a cost of £4.60 (search and extract).

If the search does not come up with your entry, you will have to pay up to £2.40 for each five-year period involved in the search.

You yourself or a representative may make a general search over any period for any number of entries on payment of the following daily rates:

In the indexes to the post-1855 BMDs	£5.00
In the parish registers pre-1855	£3.50
In the census returns 1841-1891	£3.50

If your searches are to range over more than one category, the following charges apply:

Per day or part	£6.50
Per week	£15.00
Per month	£45.00
Per quarter	£90.00

During the period of your search you may order an abstract of any entry at a cost of £2.40. You may of course copy the details down yourself without any charge over and above the search fee.

Enquiries or orders should be addressed to:

The Registrar-General for Scotland
New Register House
Edinburgh EH1 3YT

Appendix II

Names and the Ancestor-hunter

Surnames or family names have in their derivations little to offer to the ancestor-hunter. They were formed perhaps five centuries before the period that most of you will be studying. In most cases of course surnames sprang up all over Britain independently of one another. And while it is of interest to, say, the bearers of the most common surname in England and Scotland to know that the first 'Smith' was recorded in Durham, that fact has no genealogical significance whatsoever.

Even when a name is extremely localised — as in the case of one derived from an estate — this location may

have little or no significance as a link in your own searches. Historically the great clan names have strong territorial links, but the nineteenth century knew no such limits, for by then Highlanders had spread throughout Scotland and indeed the world. Certainly one would find very many Macdonalds in the Hebrides, but equally certainly your unidentified great-grandfather Donald Macdonald could have been living anywhere in Scotland from John o'Groats to Gretna Green before he left for Canada in 1860.

And as we have seen in the book, spelling conventions have nothing like the significance we attribute to them today, so the fact that you spell your name 'Miller' and not 'Millar' may have no bearing whatsoever on a grandfather who may have used either spelling — or never found any need to spell it at all.

Christian names, or more correctly given names, can on the other hand prove extremely useful to the ancestor-hunter. The Scots adopted a traditional almost ritual attitude to the naming of children. Not for them the scanning of books on Boys' Names and Girls' Names when the newcomer appeared. Babies were named after relatives and the happy couple who departed from a rigid set of priorities did so at their peril and with a great risk of family friction. The list went something like this:

Sons: 1 — father's father; 2 — mother's father; 3 — father.

Daughters: 1 — mother's mother; 2 — father's mother; 3 — mother.

This 'pecking order' as far as the naming of the new baby is concerned cannot be presented as a fixed, no-exception, formula. There were occasional regional variations, where sometimes two or even three of the people in the list bore the same name; and, sometimes, a recent death might push someone to the front of the naming queue.

Study your family's name patterns carefully, especially in the earlier years, and you will often find them giving you valuable pointers. When you come across a new name, look very hard indeed at the circumstances; it will almost certainly mean something, perhaps only the fact that a long run of boys or girls has used up the stock of traditional family Christian names.

While spelling of given names is usually more consistent than that of surnames, bear in mind that there can be variations not only in form (Ian/John, Hamish/James) but also in contractions. A Marion or an Alison may be called Mary or Ann and pass on the name to the next generation in this new form.

Today this pattern is changing and it is not so necessary to identify the many Jameses or Williams in the family by a host of additives, from Big Jimmy to Davy's Jimmie. In its place alas we have a range of strange rootless names providing variety but dissolving links.

Appendix III

The regularity of irregular marriages

Up until 1940, Scotland had a distinctive form of marriage, known rather imprecisely as an irregular marriage. This, the so-called Gretna Green marriage which lured panting English lovers north of the Border pursued by greybeard kinsmen brandishing swords, was a perfectly acceptable alternative to the conventional church wedding, involving instead a declaration in front of witnesses or before a sheriff. The epithet 'irregular' should not lead you to believe that it was illegal or second-rate (it wasn't), or that it was indulged in by a small minority: Dr Ian Grant of New Register House pointed out to me that in checking through the first 200 marriages in Glasgow Blythswood for 1904, he counted 81, more than 40 per cent, which were marriages by declaration.

By the Marriage (Scotland) Act 1939, the alternative to a church wedding became a new form of civil marriage contracted in the office and presence of certain specially authorised Registrars after publication of notice.

Appendix IV

Illegitimacy — a hurdle for the ancestor-hunter

A friend of mine started to tell me of a family tradition, but before mentioning any details he stopped and asked me to look into his forebears and see if I came up with anything unusual. Intrigued, I did as he asked and went speedily back three or four generations without a hiccup. Then I came across an ancestor who posed some problems which eventually boiled down to three different pairs of parents given on his marriage certificate, his death certificate and, after a long search, his birth certificate. And no one name appeared twice! No man has six parents, so I had to dream up some tale of passion, unrequited love and illegitimacy which coincided quite closely with the family tradition. My friend went one better by revealing that his family tradition held that none of the pairs was correct!

That was perhaps an extreme case of what illegitimacy can do to the ancestor-hunter. At the worst, it can bring an abrupt end to the male line or even in the case of a foundling to both lines, with little or no chance of further progress. At the mildest, it can introduce new elements into the search. It is quite common for ancestor-hunters to come across illegitimacy at some time. Just consider the following two instances as a sample of what you should bear in mind if your searches seem to be coming up against a brick wall:

1. A child might be born illegitimate and the mother might persuade the father to acknowledge paternity

and give the child his name. A later separation or failure to reach the altar might mean the child reverting to the mother's name or indeed acquiring the name of her future husband. Symptom: one name on the birth certificate, a second on marriage and death certificates.

2. The mother might not be able to get the father to give his name to the child and the baptismal/birth entry would be made in the mother's name. The couple might subsequently marry and legitimise the child. Symptoms: the same as previously but with the names reversed.

Appendix V

Other records in New Register House

A large part of this book has been devoted to the three great treasuries of records kept by the Registrar-General for Scotland. There are, in addition to these and to the excellent array of books on the Library shelves at New Register House, other groups of records of interest to the ancestor-hunter, the first relating to events within Scotland, the others to events outside Scotland.

1. Register of neglected entries
Births, marriages and deaths known to have occurred in Scotland between 1801 and 1854, but not included in the Old Parochial Registers.

2. Marine register of births and deaths after 1855
Births and deaths on British merchant vessels if the child's father or the deceased person was known to be Scottish. (A corresponding register exists for aircraft after 1948).

3. Service records after 1881
Births, marriages and deaths of Scottish persons serving overseas in the Armed Forces.

4. War registers from 1899
Three registers for the South African War (1899-1902), the 1914-18 War and the 1939-45 War.

5. Consular returns
Births (from 1914), marriages (from 1917) and deaths (from 1914) registered by British consuls.

6. Foreign countries
Births of children of Scottish parents, marriages and deaths of Scottish subjects, from information supplied by the parties concerned.

Appendix VI

Specialists in Family research

Mrs A. ROSEMARY BIGWOOD, M.A., M.Litt.
38 Primrose Bank Road, Edinburgh EH5 3JF.
Tel 031-552 7980

Mrs B. A. BRACK
17 Lockharton Gardens, Edinburgh EH14 1AU.
Tel 031-443 3071

Mrs DOREEN BROWN
64 Orchard Road, Edinburgh EH4 2HD.
Tel 031-332 3285

DAVID BURNS
2 Bangholm Terrace, Edinburgh EH3 5QN.
Tel 031-552 7340

Mrs K. B. CORY, F.S.A.Scot.
4 Brunstane Road, Joppa, Edinburgh EH15 2EY.
Tel 031-669 5149

Dr B.J. IGGO, Ph.D.
5 Relugas Road, Edinburgh EH9 2NE.
Tel 031-667 4879

Mrs GWEN MACLEOD
5 Bonaly Road, Edinburgh EH13 0EB.
Tel 031-441 1379

Mrs S. PITCAIRN, Mem.A.G.R.A.
106 Brucefield Avenue, Dunfermline.
Tel Dunfermline 25052

M. F. LLOYD PRICHARD, M.A., Ph.D.
36 Morton Street, Joppa, Edinburgh EH15 2HT.
Tel 031-669 4040

DANIELLA SHIPPEY, M.A.
15 Glenisla Gardens, Edinburgh EH9 2HR.
Tel 031-667 4149

Ms MARGARET SINCLAIR
83 Newington Road, Edinburgh.
Tel 031-667 0713

JAMES A. THOMSON
84 Gilmore Place, Edinburgh EH3 9PF.
Tel 031-229 3652